4

Skillful landscaping enhances contemporary buildings of concrete at the Seattle World's Fair of 1962. Architects: Walker and McGough. Photo courtesy Robert Nixon, A.I.A.

Design in Three Dimensions

Reino Randall

Associate Professor of Art, Central Washington State College, Ellensburg, Washington

Edward C. Haines

Associate Professor of Art, Central Washington State College, Ellensburg, Washington

DAVIS PUBLICATIONS, INC. • PRINTERS BUILDING • WORCESTER, MASSACHUSETTS

Acknowledgments

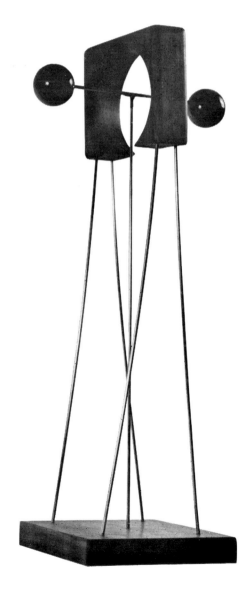

We acknowledge with pleasure and thanks the contribu-
tions of our colleagues who have encouraged us with their
enthusiasm and advice; and we are most grateful to our
former students who have shared their teaching experiences
with us. In addition, we wish to thank the professional
artists and designers whose photos we have included;
their work sets a high standard of technical competence
and expression. We are indebted, too, for the assistance of
industrial firms and travel agencies; their sense of social
responsibility is evident in their willingness to provide visual
materials and information. And finally we want to thank
our present students who have experimented endlessly
with our methods and philosophy of design.

R.R.
E.H.

Copyright 1965   •   Davis Publications, Inc.   •   Worcester, Massachusetts
Library of Congress Catalog Card Number: 65-19031
Second Printing 1967

Table of Contents

6

Foreword

Too many of us, busy with the demands of daily life, have become insensitive or indifferent to the beauty of our three-dimensional world due, no doubt, to our habit of accepting the visual world as it exists without becoming personally involved in its creation. We forget the meaning of a spatial existence until some spectacular scientific advance turns our eyes to the heavens in wonder and fear.

To reawaken our interest in the world of three dimensions we must learn to see and experience again with all the joyous eagerness of a child. One certain way to do this is to turn to the actual experience of creating with materials. This brief manual, DESIGN IN THREE DIMENSIONS, is intended to help in the search for ideas and understanding; it explains the basic probems of design and then relates the principles to functional and artistic problems. It may also be used as a source of technical information, since it provides information on materials and tools, and the illustrations from various artists and periods of history will be helpful for the ideas they suggest. These ideas and statements are not intended to be dogmatic; they are merely suggestions for the encouragement of creative students of all ages seeking to find their own personal solutions and rewards.

R.R.
E.C.H.

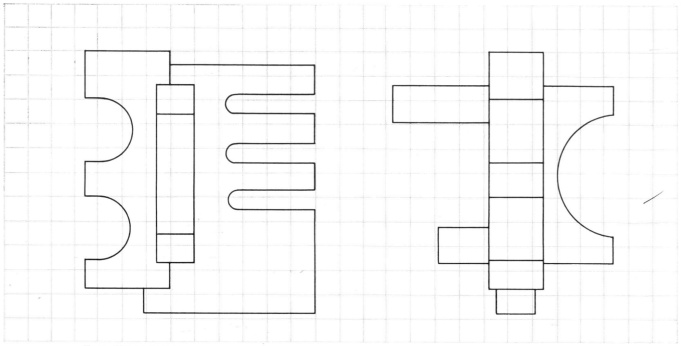

Two dimensional

What is Three-Dimensional Design?

The arts may be spatially classified in two ways: two-dimensional, *i.e.,* having only length and breadth, such as paintings, drawings and prints; any suggestion of depth must be created by illusionary devices such as perspective, color, and placement within the picture plane. The second classification, three-dimensional arts exist in space—displacing air, reflecting light, and casting shadow. Sculpture, architecture, jewelry, pottery, furniture and other crafts come within this classification.

Three dimensional

Courtesy of Ysenbourg Hoffman

Sculpture by Olivier Sequin

Why Three-Dimensional Design?

Man is a designer, never content to leave the world as he finds it; he dams the rivers, removes mountains, and builds great cities on the desert plain where none existed before. He is a creator, separating, combining, and destroying only to rebuild again in accordance with his needs. How the spatial environment is organized is of vital importance to each of us because we demand efficient use of space in a crowded world, convenience of movement, and above all, a stimulating and rich use of space in which we can develop to fullest capacity. The disappearing landscape must be replaced with a harmonious man-made environment which has not yet been achieved. Man, especially twentieth-century man, dominated by acres of concrete and steel, surrounded with gleaming buildings which obscure the sky and hide the sun, still seeks harmony with nature. It is the role of the three-dimensional designer in the fields of city planning, architecture, industrial design, and landscape to provide the order and balance which are essential to life. Yet in all probability this will not come about until education in the arts has sensitized our eyes to the potential of three-dimensional organization.

The de-humanized city needs the balance of personal, emotionalized creations which the fine arts provide. The warmth of human creation in the forms of sculpture, pottery, and other crafts can bring life to the neutral wall and cold interior—an indication that total capitulation to the machine has not occurred. The interior designer who organizes space with furniture, rugs, and accessories brings to his job the same skill and sensitivity which characterize the architect. Both professions are concerned with the arts of space.

Other artists working with materials are concerned with religious or ideological purposes, or they may attempt to solve aesthetic problems involving texture or color or perhaps they are concerned with a definition of philosophy. We approach their works with greater understanding when we are familiar with purposes and means of their expression.

A field still in need of greater understanding and imaginative approach is that of industrial design which involves the creation or improvement of products for the market. The consumer, too, having learned something about three-dimensional design, profits when he knowingly selects the best designed merchandise from the wide variety offered.

There remains yet another important value in three-dimensional art: encouragement of the non-professional to create. Many would-be producers find that the industrialized world provides every need and requirement, thereby discouraging their attempts to find pleasure in working. Often, lacking experience and technical skill, they withdraw from the very activity which provides meaning and personal involvement. Some knowlege of design and its wide potential may place within their grasp a rewarding and useful activity from which all society may profit. Such is the nature of three-dimensional art, and so great is its range of expression, that the student is assured of complete autonomy in imposing his own original order on materials he selects.

Because we are spatial beings having the characteristics of other air-displacing forms, we feel a special empathy or kinship to objects in space, and the sensuous pleasure we derive from tactile sensations reinforces our relationship to nature. We move in gardens, parks, and experience the sense of space in architecture, industrial products, and works of art. A knowledge of three-dimensional design is important to us because it can intensify our powers of perception, help us to determine quality and teach us to create in a rich, visual dimension.

Courtesy H. E. Lauffer Company.

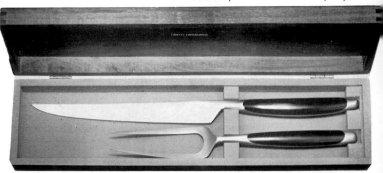

Monumental sculpture by Isamu Noguchi.
Photo courtesy First National Bank, Fort Worth, Texas.

To recognize spatial problems we must train ourselves to look at every aspect of our world. Looking closely at both man-made objects and natural forms, we compare textures and shapes for ideas applicable to three-dimensional problems. Two extremes of texture are present in this example.

Education Through Design

From childhood to adulthood sensitive awareness of three-dimensional design can be developed with an increased ability to determine good design from the mediocre or insignificant. Some of this awareness can be derived from natural experience which is recognized and clarified for us by the teacher. For example, we learn to appreciate architecture by the direct method of living in it; we learn to judge good industrial products by a sensible criteria of function, comfort, and that added quality which makes the product a joy to use. These are topics for classroom discussion at any level. Young children may be started on the path to critical awareness of their environment by a planned program which seeks to put the child into contact with good design. As a result of his school experience in talking about and working with three-dimensional materials he may respond to his physical environment in a critical way—rejecting the ugly or trivial and emphasizing what appears to be significant. The world of art will become more meaningful with each expanding experience. The student who is able to transfer his knowledge to life situations will not be content with the ugliness of an unplanned community, cheap or wasteful products, or the superficial work of art, all of which cripples his spirit and restricts his full aesthetic development.

Among the hopeful promises of the world of tomorrow is that of more leisure in which to develop our personal abilities or special talents; under such conditions the quality of human life must improve as good design and imagination determine every aspect of existence. Given an educated citizenry, sensitive to the arts, it is not unreasonable to foresee a stimulating and rewarding life which approaches ultimate human fulfilment; as teachers, our responsibility is immense.

Photo courtesy General Motors.

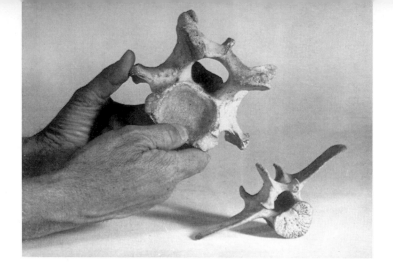

Search and Discover: Ideas from Nature and Man-Made Environment

Ideally, the artist's ideas should flow so freely that no stimulus is necessary, but in the classroom situation ideas may become inhibited. Conscious search with the help of the devices suggested in the next few pages may help to stimulate the conception of design ideas. As our inquisitive eyes search the seashore or forest, we come to the realization that nature herself provides a vast reservoir of ideas and motifs. Each natural element seems to suggest good ideas for space designs. For example, water-worn rocks, smooth and rounded, invite our hands to explore and our eyes to search. From this natural form, the idea of positive and negative composition which emphasizes sensuous delight in hand-ling may occur to the thoughtful student. Delicate grasses responding to the wind may suggest a composition as it did to the sculptor of the wire composition, page 15. Pliant branches twisting and crossing in the breeze reveal new relationships of space, and from this idea we may formulate a basic problem involving moving elements which invite new visual relation-ships as our point of vision changes.

Growing things exist in space, parts of which advance toward us and other parts recede. This fundamental principle suggests an artistic problem. With an increased consciousness of shape, texture, and space, additional ideas will spring to mind.

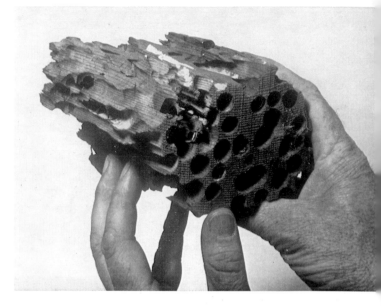

Structurally strong and light, natural shapes provide exciting curvilinear forms which suggest another problem to the inquiring student; a mass which directs the eye both inside and out in a strong rhythmical movement. To add interest and mystery the negative areas invite the eye to penetrate and explore.

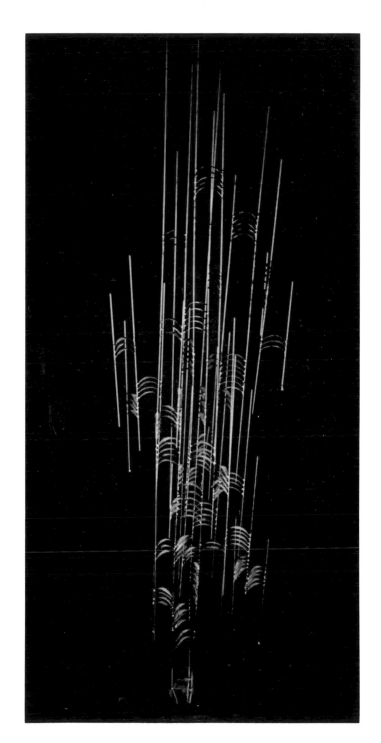

Wire Sculpture

Courtesy Japan Tourist Association.

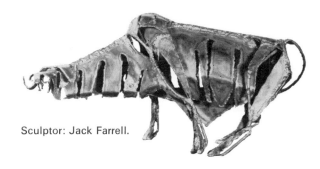

Sculptor: Jack Farrell.

With varying interpretations three artists living in different localities respond to a basic animal shape. Expressed in welded steel, the abstract qualities of mass suggested by negative and positive forms succeed in capturing a feeling of the monumental animal.

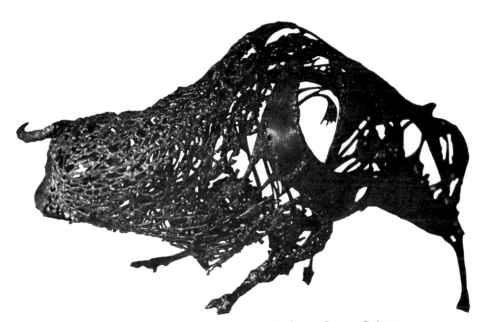

Professor George Roberts.

Sculptor: Ken Hotsko.

16

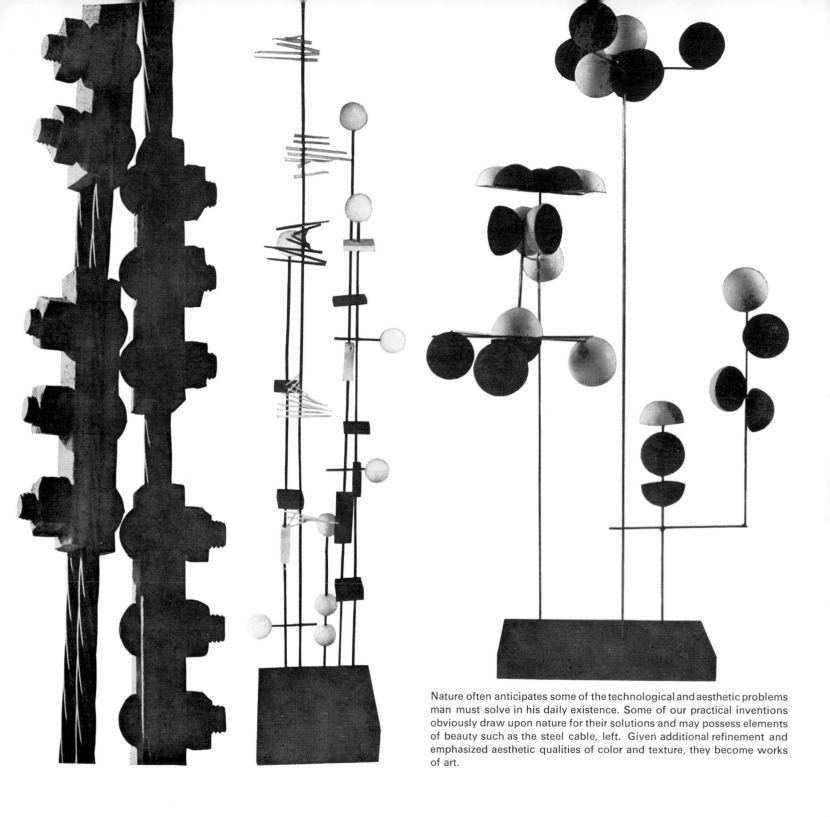

Nature often anticipates some of the technological and aesthetic problems man must solve in his daily existence. Some of our practical inventions obviously draw upon nature for their solutions and may possess elements of beauty such as the steel cable, left. Given additional refinement and emphasized aesthetic qualities of color and texture, they become works of art.

To the perceptive artist, fleeting motives such as this delicate cluster of seeds or the spiraling metal shaving caught as it arose from the lathe, stimulate ideas for sculpture which may possess deep meaning and significance.

"When the nozzles around the perimeter of the lagoon shoot jets of water at its base," says Bertoia, "it gives the effect of a beautiful flower rising out of the primeval mist—sort of a representation of the beginning of life itself." An outstanding fountain by Harry Bertoia, nationally-famous sculptor.

Photo courtesy Perpetual Savings and Loan Association, Beverly Hills, California.

Finding in nature a source of inspiration, artists throughout the ages have studied her forms as point of departure for their own work. To sketch an object requires close scrutiny and analysis; the art student should cultivate the sketch book habit as a means of storing ideas and information.

1. Stained with wood stains, natural driftwood required imagination and some refinement with tools to bring it to realization as an abstract bird form.

2. The artist derived his basic ideas from living rock reliefs. The material is easy to manage soft-soldered zinc. The essential difference between natural and man-made form is the selectivity and organization motivated by human intelligence and emotion.

3. The bandsaw or jigsaw is the tool which frees the curvilinear forms from a 2 x 10 fir plank. By projecting sections, strong shadows and lights are created to reveal the course of the idea in nature.

1.

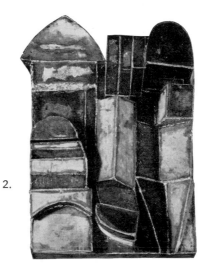

2.

Photo courtesy Mrs. Joy Wilson.

3.

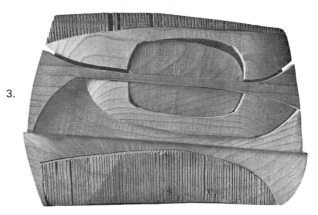

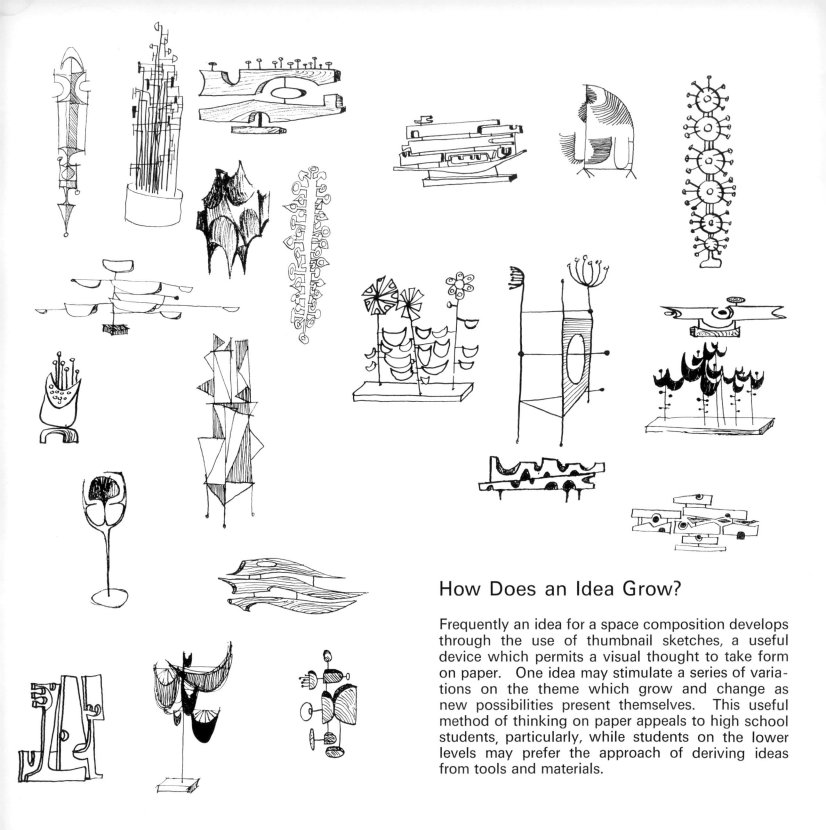

How Does an Idea Grow?

Frequently an idea for a space composition develops through the use of thumbnail sketches, a useful device which permits a visual thought to take form on paper. One idea may stimulate a series of variations on the theme which grow and change as new possibilities present themselves. This useful method of thinking on paper appeals to high school students, particularly, while students on the lower levels may prefer the approach of deriving ideas from tools and materials.

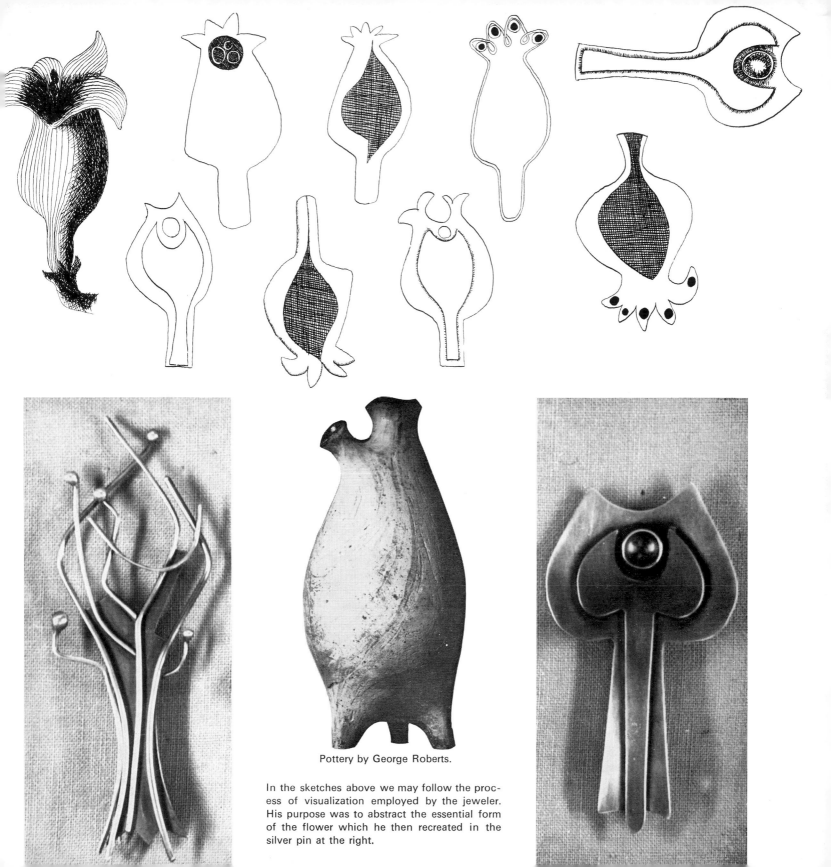

Pottery by George Roberts.

In the sketches above we may follow the process of visualization employed by the jeweler. His purpose was to abstract the essential form of the flower which he then recreated in the silver pin at the right.

Search and Discover:
Ideas from Tools and Materials

Not all ideas spring directly from imagination, complete and meaningful; some are suggested by the manipulation of tools and materials. Working without a preconceived plan the artist may find his idea developing from the nature of the quality of his material, such as wire and wood casually combined in a spirit of playful handling. From the physical act of bending, twisting and shaping, the fertile imagination will sense possibilities of three-dimensional designs.

Tools and their characteristic marks are also a means of conceiving an idea, because each tool leaves its path of action on the material due to its construction and use. The difference between two kinds of pliers illustrates the difference of effects. The needle nose pliers makes small, curved bends while the broad pliers with flat edges give a more rigid angle. The ball-peen hammer leaves an antique texture on smooth wood or metal. Rasps, files, and planes make recognizable tool marks. The power tools provide a wide variety of effects; the table saw, jig-saw, or band saw are useful tools for the large studio. Knowledge of tools and their uses expands one's working vocabulary of effects.

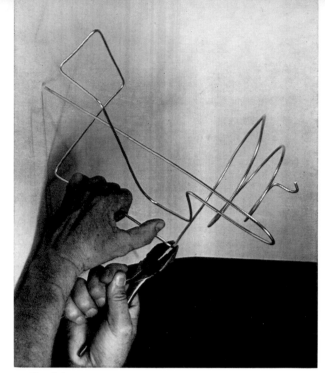

The inherent qualities of soft aluminum wire will dictate its final form. It may be bent at right angles or gracious curves; it is strong yet pliable. If the student respects its nature, he will not distort this linear material into inappropriate forms.

A natural gray driftwood form, nails, wire, and beach pebbles all securely glued, capture the lyrical feeling of the sea. The rhythmic design and subdued color express the spirit of beach, sand, and sky.

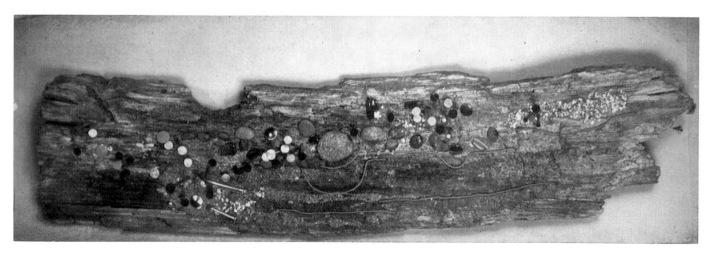

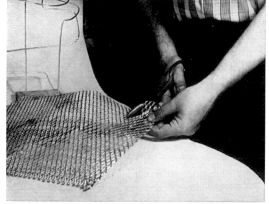

1. Working with paper, tape, scissors, and pins, small models of the project are easily created before the student begins his project in aluminum or cardboard. Many projects are appropriate in heavy drawing paper at all levels.

2. Tinsnips and plaster wire lath are not difficult to handle at the Junior and Senior high school levels. The material may be wired together and painted with enamels. The bent materials will suggest mobiles or standing sculpture.

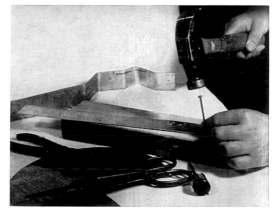

3. With hammer and nails an endless variety of textures are formed to add interest to the project.

4. At the Junior and Senior high school levels, the solder gun is an intriguing tool which creates textural pattern and serves as an indispensable method of fastening. Constant supervision is required to prevent injury.

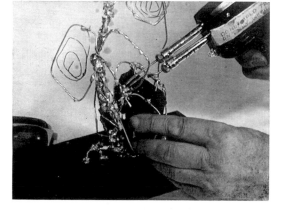

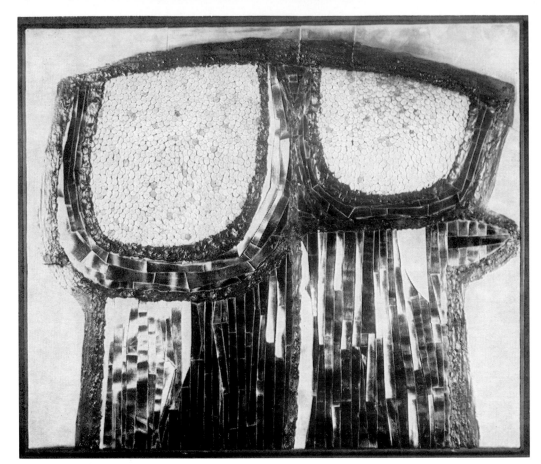

1.

Artist: Darwin Davis.

2.

Sculpture by Darwin Davis.

3.

5.

4.

1. A low relief on an aluminum background. Strips of metal cut from tin cans and adhered with aluminum liquid vary the color from gray to copper. Textured areas are formed by overlapped shingle nails driven into the background.

2. Wood relief with large and small forms securely adhered with glue. Natural wood colors present a restrained effect.

3. With a wire staple as a holder for hanging, this sawdust and wallpaper paste sculpture is enhanced with water paints. See recipe, p. 45

4. Massive and strong in appearance, wood blocks carefully formed and adjusted on the bandsaw are assembled and glued. An effective work in strong light and shadow.

5. Using a small box as a container, fine wet sand is carved in the negative. Liquid plaster-of-Paris is then poured into the mould which reverses the composition. Concrete is a more permanent material for outdoor use.

1.

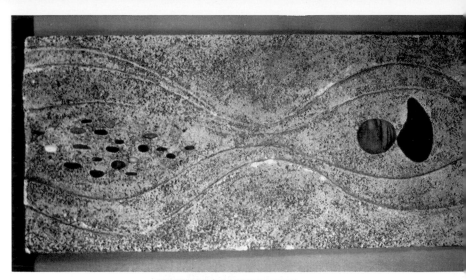

Search and Discover:
Ideas from Emotions

Thoughts and feelings are a rich source of ideas which may be expressed in three-dimensional design. We attempt to express these feelings in symbolic form with a knowledge of the emotional meanings of color, texture, form, line, and space. The horizontal line direction may express rest or repose; a diagonal suggests movement and activity; a vertical line conveys the feeling of exultation, vitality or lifting up. The dropping form, the erect form, the closely spaced form or empty and vacant forms are useful symbols, usually interpreted intuitively by the viewer. Forms may be rigid or soft and yielding; the feelings conveyed by a multiplicity of small forms differ from that of large simple shapes. Open areas are light and airy; mass is heavy and depressive. Texture and color add their meaning to ideas conceived from our emotions.

3.

1. Cast stone (concrete and m chips) expresses a secure and feeling by its mass and con contour.

2. Cast cement (sand casting riched by beach pebbles conv lyrical and gentle emotion ren ing us of waves.

3. Wire and eggcrate forms su still another feeling—lightness, and joy.

28

What is a Collage?

Braque and Picasso are given the credit for the invention of a new kind of sculpture which extended the limited range of traditional relief and in-the-round sculpture. Using the common materials available in their studios such as shingles, string, paper and other textured materials strongly adhered to a background, the new relief departed from realistic values to express new meanings for the 20th century. Materials usually not associated with sculpture were presented directly to the spectator in a frank revelation of color and texture. The shock of the new sculpture forced the viewer to consider new definitions of art and to realize that esthetic qualities were more important than realistic subject matter and story. Painted and stenciled areas add interest to the collage.

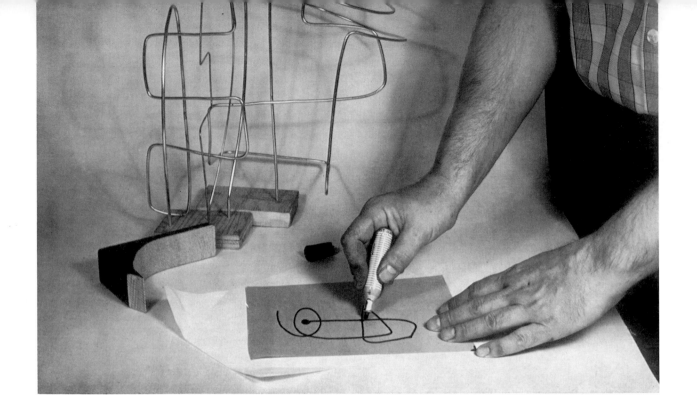

Search and Discover:
Ideas from Spontaneous Sketching

To the student searching for an idea, the free and spontaneous meanderings of the brush or pencil, undirected and playful in approach, may provide a source. Various patterns either softly flowing and lyrical or rigidly geometric, such as superimposed rectangles, may stimulate ideas but once a shape emerges from the pencil, intelligence takes over to correct, change, evaluate, and perhaps to discard if the ideas are unpromising. Areas may be darkened or transposed as desired. One useful method to handle a sketch for transfer or correction is to make a rubbed transfer on a second sheet of paper or the original may be placed against the window for tracing. Materials are important; soft charcoal for transfers, crayon, the brush and paint, all encourage free movement and invention.

The world around us may prompt the imagination when we begin to see possibilities in nature's own design: the tangle of shrubbery against the sky or the patterns made by moving things in fresh snow.

1.

1. and 2.   The Japanese brush or soft charcoal offers little resistance to free movement and responds readily to the promptings of imagination when the artist seeks new forms.

3.   To find possibilities in scrap material and to sense the eventual result of merging color and form require skillful habits of seeing, but once formed, this ability transfers to other visual problems and becomes one of the artist's most valuable skills.

2.

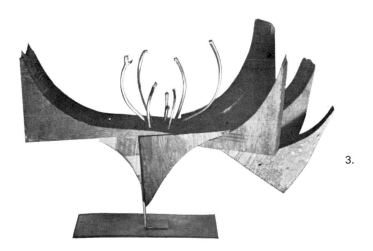

3.

Search and Discovery: Ideas From the Art of the Past and Present

Often ideas present themselves to our minds as we wander through art galleries and museums, or when we examine magazines and newspapers. We observe that artists throughout the ages have solved their problems in the materials available to them and in harmony with the artistic theories of their own day. Considering the needs of his society, he may choose to emphasize dramatic color for ritual purposes or he may be called upon to simplify and distort shapes to carry the ideas of the spiritual. Artists of our times, seeking new forms and new meaning, have found new leads in the works of the past. Modigliani, for example, was impressed with the vigor of the primitive distortions of African masks; Gauguin rediscovered new ideas in the sculpture and relief of the ancient Egyptians and Cambodians.

All cultures have considered three-dimensional objects essential to their existence. Their unique social and religious requirements included architecture, which served as tombs, homes, or temples; sculpture, which symbolized spiritual forces or served as reminders of the departed; while jewelry and

Rose Window, Santa Maria Maggiote, Tuscania, Italy. Photo courtesy Hans Bellmann.

weapons served their obvious purposes. Usually these objects were conceived with great sensitivity to material and form. Today these works of art express a mode of handling form, space, texture, line, and color which may point the way to a more expressive, contemporary statement of three-dimensional art.

Photo courtesy Everett Jr. College.

The line, spiral and circle, all universal motives, appear in traditional and contemporary adaptations expressed in a wide variety of materials—sandcastings, paper and wood.

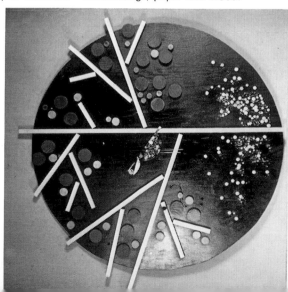

A traditional Northwest totem carved in cedar by Charlie James, a noted Kwakiutl Indian.

Sculpture by Harold Balasz in the Norton Building, Seattle, Washington. Architects: Bindon and Wright.

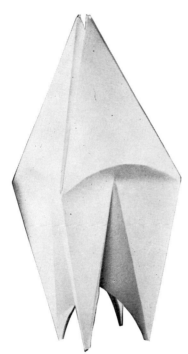

The totem pole is found among several primitive peoples, chief of these being the Oceanic peoples and the North-west Coast Indian. Using the idea of a superimposed form arranged vertically, contemporary artists find the same problem challenging. Related through light and shadow and color, each part of the totem pole retains its importance and encourages examination, but the total design of all the parts dominates. The idea of self-containment or respect for the original pole form is also a compositional factor. The cut and folded paper compositions were suggested by traditional Japanese lanterns, and ancient stone sculpture.

Courtesy Milton F. Sullivan.

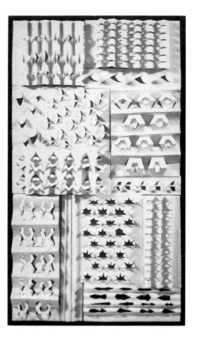

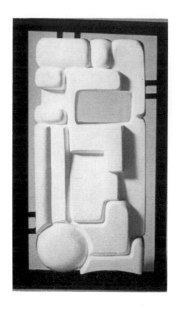

The city museum is a good source of information as these careful sketches reveal. We look to the shapes, materials used, and the organization of all the visual elements. From ideas found in primitive works of sculpture, the artists, working in plaster and wood, explored variations in shapes.

Each cultural group has a unique way of handling the visual elements. One group may stress mass, or another may stress negative relationships; these habitual ways of working we call style. These examples illustrate an abstract style based on natural forms highly simplified, distorted, or exaggerated in order to convey the artist's special meaning. An abstraction is an attempt to portray the true reality of the object devoid of the superficial.

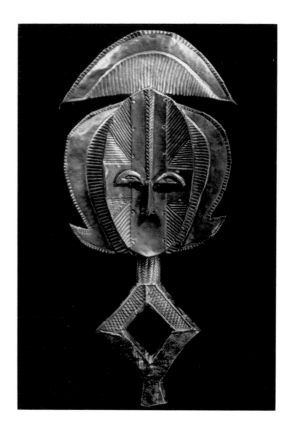

Mayan slate bowl, from the Yucatan, left, and reliquary figure, above, brass over wood, from Gabun, Bakota tribes, Africa.   Courtesy Seattle Art Museum.

a.

b.

c.

d.

a. Akua'ba Fertility image, wood, Ashanti, Africa.

b. Aztec God of Flowers, volcanic rock.

c. Spirit antelope headdress, Bambara tribe, wood, Africa.

d. Head, terra cotta, Benin, Africa.

e. Figure of wood, Sepik River, New Guinea.

All photos courtesy Seattle Art Museum.

e.

CONTEMPORARY SCULPTURE is too often an irritating puzzle to the public who look for non-artistic values and story content in works of art. In the past, when the artist relied on accurate drawing and modeling, natural color, and perspective to convey his communication, the "imitation of nature" criteria provided the lay public some basis for judging art, but the modern artist having mastered visual space and anatomy no longer attempts to transcribe superficial appearance. With a new appreciation of the esthetics of sculpture: line, texture, form, mass, space, and light, he may stress content or meaning drawn from all sources. Frequently his work represents a special esthetic problem without a profound meaning.

Some sculptors have declared their total independence of tradition to take advantage of the materials of our time as symbols of our industrial society: steel, plastic, glass, and discarded materials, composed according to the laws of chance. Their non-figural forms, expressed in a highly subjective idiom, further widen the breach between artist and public.

Whether the sculptor bases his work on abstracted natural form or non-figural shapes, we discover upon study that its message is pertinent and illuminating. Moreover, we find that the contemporary sculptor is no less sensitive nor skilled than great artists of other ages. To reject contemporary sculpture without an attempt to understand its meaning for our time is to deprive ourselves of a stimulating emotional and intellectual comment on contemporary life.

Sculptor: Harold Balasz.

a.

b.

Choosing a Material for Your Idea

Our own environment supplies us with various kinds of material, each with its characteristic physical limitations and possibilities. To discover what a material is capable of doing, we work experimentally with a variety of tools. We discover that wire has certain characteristics of "bendability" and strength that make it appropriate for one use and not another, or that wood is rigid but does not convey the feeling of softness. A sensitivity to materials will teach us the emotional meanings which each possesses and will reinforce our intentions to convey a certain meaning. For example, clay which is soft and yielding, suggests a fluid or lyrical approach appropriate to round and gentle forms while stone is hard and rigid with an added meaning of endurance and permanency. The wider our acquaintance with materials, the greater our expressive vocabulary. But mere experimentation should not become the aim of the classroom project; personal expression and the satisfaction of a complete project are more important.

What the artist accomplishes with material is more important than the material itself. Scrap wood, wire or plastic found in every school storeroom, may be used in such a way that it raises the material to the level of meaningful art. Sensitivity to the materials around us is one of the logical and desirable outcomes of working with three-dimensional design.

40

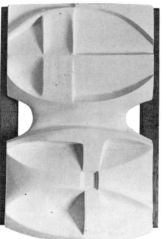

a. For cutting curved and straight line patterns the coping saw and jigsaw, for the lower grades, and the bandsaw for more advanced students are important tools. Contrasts of color, texture, and material are revealed in the artist's choice of wood and cork.

b. To emphasize problems in structure, balsa wood, available at local craft shops, is both easy to work and strong. Additional color and texture are provided by colored papers glued to the surfaces.

c. Within a wooden frame which has been perforated with a small hand drill, string tensions pull from side to side creating overlapping planes and colors. Inside this limited spatial area suspended paper forms create focal points. A cardboard box, fine wire, yarn, or string may be substituted.

d. A multicolored paper box relief illustrates advancing and receding planes. A basic architectural problem is the organization of volumes and forms with consideration given to the play of light and dark. Paper boxes or folded paper forms may be used successfully to create a variety of original designs.

e. and f. Plaster of Paris, one of the most satisfactory carving materials, requires minimum equipment and may be purchased locally. Before carving the plaster the mass should be dampened. To prevent dusting, liquid floor wax may be brushed on the completed sculpture.

The Materials, the Source, the Project

Metals (sheet)

aluminum (*JS*)
copper (*JS*)
steel (*JS*)
galvanized tin, zinc, tin, iron (*JS*)

Cans

galvanized (*EJS*)
aluminum (*JS*)
stove pipe (*EJS*)
drain pipe (*JS*)
toothpaste tubes (*EJS*)

Wire

stovepipe wire (*EJS*)
copper wire (*EJS*)
aluminum wire (*EJS*)
steel wire (*EJS*)
piano wire (*JS*)
model airplane wire (*EJS*)
screen wire (*EJS*)
hardware cloth (*EJS*)
welding rod (*JS*)
  brass
  bronze
expanded metal lathe (*JS*)
coat hangers (*JS*)
springs (*EJS*)
baling wire (*EJS*)
clothesline (*EJS*)

Wood

plywood (various dimensions, kinds) (*EJS*)
solid stock (*EJS*)

Easy to work woods

pine (*EJS*)
mahogany (*EJS*)
cedar (*EJS*)
balsa (*EJS*)

Scrap woods

apple boxes (*EJS*)
bushel baskets (*EJS*)
mill ends (*EJS*)
cheese boxes (*EJS*)
doweling (*EJS*)
children's toy blocks (*EJS*)
construction toys (*EJS*)
driftwood (*EJS*)
toothpicks, plain and colored (*EJS*)

Clay

oil-base clay (non-firing type) (*EJS*)
potter's clay: red, white, buff (*EJS*)
buff (*EJS*)
brick clay (*EJS*)
river or creek clay (*EJS*)

3.

Treatment of clay

glazes (*EJS*)
waxed (*EJS*)
fired (*EJS*)
mosaic clay tile (*EJS*)

1. Soft-soldered wire

2. Wood scraps glued to background

3. Fired clay figure

4. Ping-pong balls and copper wire

5. Corrugated cardboard

6. Colored glass and liquid steel

7. Straws, colored paper and foil

1.

2.

Plastic

styrofoam (*EJS*)
sheets (*EJS*)
balls (*EJS*)
drinking cups (*EJS*)
acrylic (*JS*)
lucite (*JS*)
fiberglass (*JS*)
casting resin (*JS*)
  (available at hardware,
  paint stores)
corrugated and plain in a
  variety of colors (*JS*)
theatrical gelatin (*EJS*)
  (great range of colors,
  theatrical supply houses)
cellophane in colored
  sheets (*EJS*)

4.

Plastic miscellaneous

ping-pong balls (*EJS*)
toothpicks, colored (*EJS*)
containers:
  detergent (*EJS*)
  cosmetic (*EJS*)
  coffee can lids (*EJS*)

Paper

construction (*EJS*)
newsprint (*EJS*)
Japanese:
  tissue paper (*EJS*)
  origami (*EJS*)
  rice paper (*EJS*)
  mulberry paper (*EJS*)
  metallic (*EJS*)
oatmeal (*EJS*)
facial tissue (*EJS*)
cellophane (*EJS*)
aluminum foil (*EJS*)
parchment (*EJS*)

Containers

boxes, cardboard (*EJS*)
corrugated (*EJS*)
mailing tubes (*EJS*)
powder boxes (*EJS*)
clothes boxes (*EJS*)
hat boxes (*EJS*)
oatmeal, salt, and egg
  boxes (*EJS*)
cardboard (*EJS*)
illustration board (*EJS*)
tag board (*EJS*)
excelsior (*EJS*)
packing material (*EJS*)
wax paper (*EJS*)
crepe paper (*EJS*)
wallpaper (*EJS*)
wrapping paper (*EJS*)
butcher paper (*EJS*)

5.

Glass

window (*JS*)
antique (*JS*)
stained (*JS*)
bottle glass (*JS*)
art glass in chunks (consult
  glass stores) (*JS*)
tile glass (*JS*)
smalto (*JS*)
tesserae (tile) (*JS*)
  (from any tile store)

6.

How to Fasten

dowels, glue (*JS*)
epoxy (*JS*)
liquid metals and liquid
  aluminum in tubes (*JS*)
household cement, regular
  and fast dry (*JS*)
contact cement (*JS*)
rubber cement (*JS*)
iron glue (*JS*)
resin glue (*JS*)
plastic glue (*JS*)
solder (*JS*)
nails and screws (*EJS*)
wiggle nails (*EJS*)
bolts (*EJS*)
staples (*EJS*)
paste (*EJS*)
  (above available at
  hardware stores)

7.

Miscellaneous

cork (*EJS*)
linoleum (*EJS*)
masonite (*EJS*)
screen (*EJS*)
asbestos (*EJS*)
pebbles and sand (*EJS*)
found objects (*EJS*)
toothpicks (*EJS*)
straws (*EJS*)
pressboard (*EJS*)
yarn (*EJS*)
string (*EJS*)
fishline (*EJS*)
thread (*EJS*)
soap (*EJS*)
paraffin (*EJS*)
wax (*EJS*)
plaster and cement (*JS*)

What Can You Do With Materials?

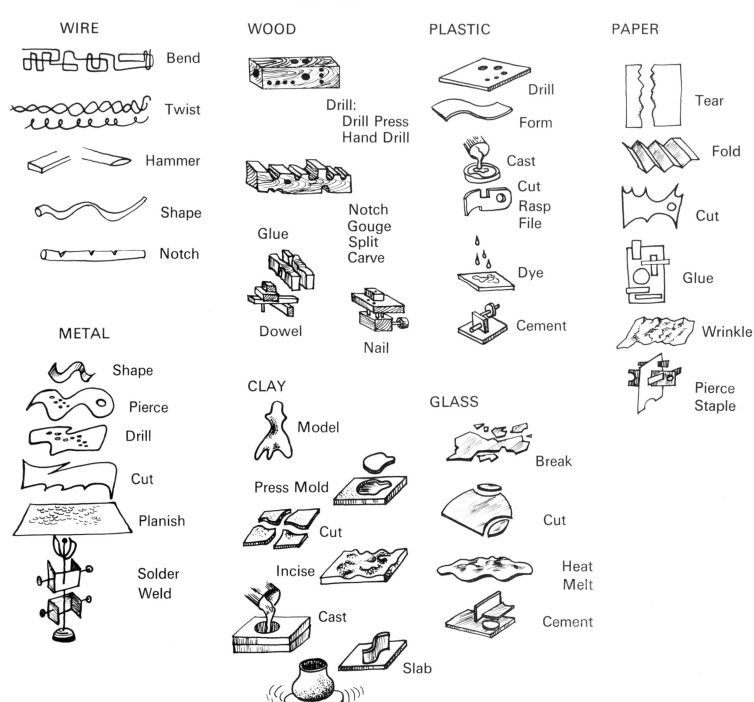

WIRE
Bend
Twist
Hammer
Shape
Notch

WOOD
Drill:
Drill Press
Hand Drill
Notch
Gouge
Split
Carve
Glue
Dowel
Nail

PLASTIC
Drill
Form
Cast
Cut
Rasp
File
Dye
Cement

PAPER
Tear
Fold
Cut
Glue
Wrinkle
Pierce
Staple

METAL
Shape
Pierce
Drill
Cut
Planish
Solder
Weld

CLAY
Model
Press Mold
Cut
Incise
Cast
Slab
Throw

GLASS
Break
Cut
Heat
Melt
Cement

Recipes for Modeling and Carving Materials

PAPIER-MACHE PULP

Tear newspaper into small pieces and soak in water for 48 hours. Drain water and mix with wheat paste or flour. Add Oil of Cloves to retard fermentation. Model over armature such as wire or bottle. May require gentle heat to dry. Paint with oil or water-base colors.

SAWDUST AND PASTE

Mix sawdust and dry wheat paste (about two sawdust to one paste), then add water. Material can be modeled over armature. Paint.

SAWDUST AND PLASTER

Mix equal parts of sawdust and dry plaster, adding water to desired consistency. Pour into oatmeal or milk carton. Use opaque water color to tint mixture. When set, may be carved with tools. Paint.

PLASTER OF PARIS

Mix about ¾ pound of plaster to one quart of cold water. Pour into box form or carton. When hard, may be carved with tools, or when totally dry, remoistened for easy carving. Caution: do not pour plaster into sink. Finished work may be painted with water-base paints or shellacked before painting with oil-base colors. Or wax.

ASBESTOS, PLASTER, AND CEMENT

1 part cement, 1 part plaster, 2 parts absestos, add water to paste consistency. Apply to wire or metal armature. May be carved when dry. Add surface texture and color as desired. Color mixture with wood stains.

CEMENT

Mix 2 parts cement with 1 part water, stir to consistency of thick cream, add color if desired (mineral colors available at most paint stores). Pour into prepared plaster mould and jar to remove air bubbles. Let set for 24 to 48 hours. Good for sand casting technique or prepared plaster moulds. For additional information, see bibliography.

PLASTER AND VERMICULITE

Mix equal parts of vermiculite and plaster in dry state; add water and stir to consistency of thick paste. Pour into cardboard forms (milk cartons, oatmeal boxes, etc.). Let harden and carve. May be remoistened when dry.

Language of Design

VOLUME: Interior space like that of a teacup.

TENSION: A pulling or strain between forms, textures, or other parts of a composition.

MOVEMENT: As our inquiring eyes follow the flow of shapes (forms) we experience the sensation of movement which is a direction or projection of vision indicated by line, color, space, or texture.

MASS: Solidity of form which seems permanent and massive.

BIOMORPHIC FORM: Shapes derived from living things.

RELIEF: Sculpture which projects from the background, to be seen only from the front and sides.

POSITIVE AND NEGATIVE SHAPES: A negative is a void, a hole or open area; positive forms exist as substance.

LINE: Line does not exist in nature but we interpret edges or contour as line. A shape may be compact and closed, or spiny, rough and open. We relate ourselves to line and tend to move with it.

PLANE: A facet or face of form.

CONCAVE: Recessed areas which pull back from our vision, usually curved and hollow.

CONVEX: Advancing areas, the opposite of concavity, a bulging curved surface.

FORM: There are two basic meanings of form: total organization of all parts including structure; or the word may indicate shapes, either two-dimensional or three-dimensional. Forms may be geometric, biomorphic, or representational.

SPACE: All three-dimensional arts involve space, which may be thought of as void. Three-dimensional arts exist in width, length, and depth, displace air, reflect light and cast shadows.

IN-THE-ROUND: Sculpture which is intended to be viewed from all sides, front and back.

COLOR: Color or polychromy in three-dimensional design is traditionally limited to neutral grays and tans or the natural colors of the material, but it can become one of the most expressive elements when used with imagination. To convey feelings of broad scope a wide range of color including unusual combinations should be attempted. When used to augment advancing and receding space polychromed parts are useful.

TEXTURE: Texture or tactile surface quality is important in this area of design. The roughness or smoothness of surface may be conveyed through the use of touch, or solely through visual means. Tool marks and the indigenous quality of the material, screen wire, or soft velvet, contribute eye appeal as well as hand appeal.

Visual Glossary (Vocabulary)

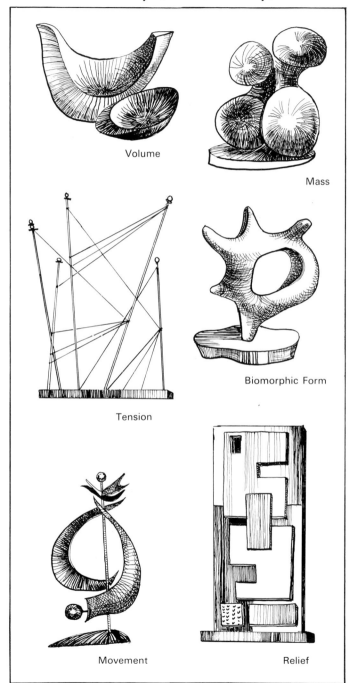

Volume

Mass

Tension

Biomorphic Form

Movement

Relief

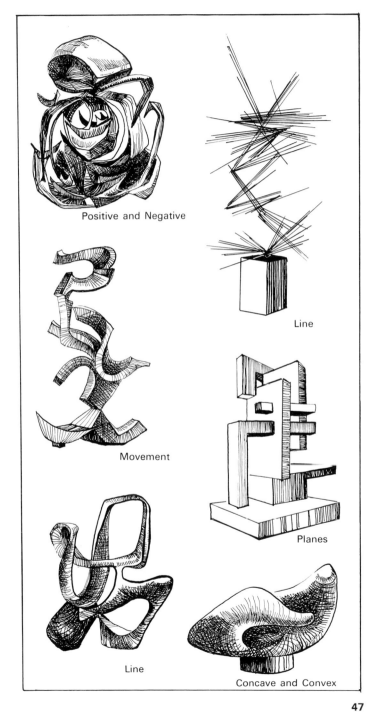

Positive and Negative

Line

Movement

Planes

Line

Concave and Convex

Light and Shadow

An important esthetic element which must be carefully considered by the three-dimensional designer is the revealing play of light and dark. By projecting parts or permitting certain planes to recede into space, shadows of various qualities are formed; they may be dense or transparent according to the artist's purpose. Light and shadow may function in various ways; textures may be emphasized, contours defined, or fulness of mass stressed as illustrated below. Surface enrichment of any kind, either raised pattern or recessed areas, are made to function by the kind of light chosen to illuminate the work. Textured relief sculpture which tends to flatness may give the illusion of greater depth by side or overhead lighting; sculpture in the round is fully realized by back lighting. In order to grasp the effectiveness of buildings and outdoor sculpture it is necessary to study the works throughout the day under changing conditions of light.

1.

2.

3.

1. The subtle, granular surface of the plaster is brought to our attention by brilliant illumination.
2. Edges or contours are dramatically stated by backlighting and reveal their importance in the total design. 3. Strong light and shadow indicate massive forms which both project and recede.

Design Criteria

No artist ever works without pausing from time to time to consider what he has accomplished in light of his purpose. His criteria or personal system of evaluation may be vague and not easily expressed in words but he senses his strength and weakness. Few artists living in the same age and country agree entirely on a set of values; criteria vary from artist to artist and from period to period since art is not subject to specific and unchangeable laws. Are there any general principles by which to evaluate three-dimensional art? One such principle which seems to be generally accepted is the quality of vitality which is able to transform inert stone, clay, or wood into a dynamic, life-like creation. It comes about through intense personal involvement with ideas and materials; it is a quality which is transmitted from the artist himself and represents a bit of his own life. Expressive vitality, then, is an important criteria which most people recognize as an essential quality of any art form.

Within the broad boundaries set up by culture, a style of working and available materials, artists agree on other general principles but no work will conform in every detail. The personal way of handling mass, volume, light, dark, and space relationships in necessary violations of a criteria, give art the sparkle of surprise. Any narrow views which refuse to admit that art is a projection of personality limit our appreciation and enjoyment. Since we cannot establish an absolute criteria of art even if it were desirable, the beginning student may think of the following points as guides and only guides:

LIGHT AND DARK:
... does the sculptural composition take advantage of its three-dimensional nature in relation to lights, darks, shadows (either artificial or natural light)?

TEXTURE:
... will texture increase richness and focus attention on specific areas?

EXPRESSION:
... are the ideas original, fresh and used in a personal way?
... is the composition expressive of our times, both physically and spiritually?
... is the composition meaningful, intellectually or emotionally?

MATERIAL:
... are materials used to exploit qualities of color, texture, or structural strength?
... is the material appropriate for the problem?

CRAFTSMANSHIP:
... is the sculpture well made; does it "hold together"?
... is it structurally strong; does it hang or balance evenly?
... are details carefully considered?

SPACE:
... are the space relationships carefully considered; are there contrasts of large and small spaces?
... is the composition consistent?

USE:
... is the sculptural work appropriate to its site?
... is the quality of the sculpture in harmony with its purpose?

Sculpture by Professor George Roberts.

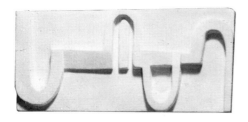

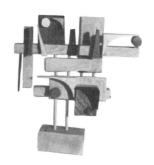

The quality of imagination stimulated by the class instructor, the wide variety of materials used, and the various kinds of problems solved prove that three-dimensional design can be handled successfully by the average student. Given materials and a few basic tools students at all levels can create space compositions which have meaning both as art expression and as learning devices.

Architecture as Three-Dimensional Design

Good architecture, like any other expressive art such as painting or sculpture, is a summary of what a people believe and a way of life expressed in permanent three-dimensional material—clay, steel or glass. Tourists in foreign countries still thrill to the glories of ancient buildings when the feeling of the culture is expressed in the quality of the design. The massing of parts, the use of interior space, building decoration or enhancement, and structural problems all carry a meaning to the perceptive viewer. Throughout the ages the motivations or reasons for building have stated the nature of the culture. Some cultures were preoccupied with religious faith as is evident in Egyptian temples or Gothic churches, but in ancient Rome, the stress is placed on amphitheaters and great public buildings intended to impress a restless population with governmental strength and prosperity. Sculpture and architecture are closely related in their esthetics. Buildings with their broad surfaces reflect and absorb light, a factor carefully considered by the architect who uses dark shadows and highlights as part of the design. One problem in architecture requires the unifying of large areas through the use of light and dark. Windows, doors, cornices, and pediments become textural patterns in the total concept of design.

The widest variety of materials have been used for buildings. Aside from structural use, a determining reason for choice of material lies in its textural effect, a factor in relating the building to its purpose and site. Some architects like Frank Lloyd Wright have insisted that materials be carefully related to site in terms of color and texture in order to integrate large man-made masses with nature. We add interest and enjoyment to buildings by planning for the effective use of color. Added contrasts of both color and texture are assured by the combination of materials.

Like sculpture, architecture invites our wandering eyes to investigate its exterior mass and to penetrate interior space or volume. In ancient buildings the idea of mass seems to dominate with only a hint of the interior suggested by doors and windows, but in contemporary architecture interior space is suggested and emphasized. By opening walls through large uses of glass, interior volume which carries the idea of living space dominates the idea of the structure. In a successful building our impressions of exterior and interior merge into an integrated whole as we move from area to area. Architecture in this contemporary sense is closely related to modern concepts of sculptural space. A student of three-dimensional design is well prepared to appreciate and to make effective use of architecture.

Courtesy Robinson's Department Store; sculpture by George Tsutakawa.

Against an intense blue sky, a ribbed tower of natural stone rises from its luxuriant setting. Surrounded by trees, flowers and vines it echoes the nature of its habitat in the rich play of light and shadow. It is organic in its concept of design, material and site, and so harmonious that sculpture and architecture lose their separate identity to merge in a total three-dimensional expression. Qutb Minar, Delhi, India. Photo courtesy Government of India.

Night view of the Johnson's Wax research and development tower in Racine, Wisconsin. Like a giant candle the bands of light pass through 17 miles of hollow glass tubing which circle the 156-foot tower. Between the glass are bands of brick. Note how the building is supported on the narrow hollow shaft which is only 13 feet at the narrowest point. Photo courtesy Johnson's Wax.

Humayun's Tomb, Delhi.
The solidity of this massive building is relieved by the small
windows and shadow-catching arches. Color and pattern
add Oriental richness to the tomb. Courtesy Government
of India.

In this contemporary church our eyes soar upward with the direction of the laminated arches, and we experience a kinetic response, and a sense of exultation, an emotional effect planned by the architect. Courtesy National Lumber Manufacturers Association.

The mass of the upper structure rests lightly on its steel piers in this contemporary home designed by David McKinley of Seattle, Washington. Courtesy Bethlehem Steel.

Main entrance to the Central Restaurant of General Motors Technical Center. At the right is a metal screen designed by the noted sculptor, Harry Bertoia. Courtesy General Motors Technical Center.

Interior photo of display at Milano.
Related to the interior of this contemporary building are the straight-line and simple furnishings combining rich color and texture. Photo courtesy Publifoto, Milan.

The four modules or units in the American Home of the Immediate Future are arranged around a central courtyard allowing easy passage from room, each of which contains built-in heating, air-conditioning, plumbing, and lighting requirements. Courtesy United States Plywood Corp.

Space problem for a family of four is solved in the four-module American Home of the Immediate Future, designed by Robert M. Engelbrecht, A.I.A. Courtesy United States Plywood Corp.

The living room of the Plywood house has sliding doors looking into the central courtyard, thus uniting both interior and exterior. Courtesy United States Plywood Corp.

A large interior space is effectively divided by a screen which permits the eye to penetrate into the spaces beyond, yet defines a specific area of activity; a good example of cooperation between artist and architect. Screen designed by James Fitzgerald for the Seattle Public Library. Roger Dudley, photographer.

Architecture has often been called the "mother of the arts" because it has employed sculpture and painting as necessary enhancement. The fine arts working in harmony with a building help to bring it to completion and perfection, thus becoming integrated parts of the whole. Relief sculpture dramatically illuminated, playing fountains in secluded gardens or courts, or sculpture-in-the-round placed before a handsome wall add enrichment and humanization to a satisfying environment for man. Courtesy La Jolla Federal Savings and Loan Association. Julius Shulmann, photographer.

Design in Industrial Design

The entire field of industrial design is involved in our study of three-dimensional design and the comfort and convenience of modern living are directly related to the success of our industrial designers. Without them contemporary life which leans so heavily on the abundance of machine-made products could hardly be carried on. Mass production has placed within the reach of every person the essentials for a satisfying material life: furniture, automobiles, homes, and tools of all kinds. It has released man from burden and given him an opportunity to develop to his fullest capacity. But at the same time it has imposed new and restrictive forces upon his potential because it has multiplied the ''gimick'', the cheap imitation and the wasteful.

Since our lives in a machine culture depend upon machine-made objects, every aspect of life is affected and our responsibility to choose and to make use of well-designed products is increased. The sensitivity gained from handling materials and tools, of seeing, discussing, and evaluating good industrial products can raise the standard of our civilization. Good design as a way of life will come about when we demand it. Manufacturers who are conscious of the power of public opinion have immense social responsibilities to help create an esthetic and sensitive citizenry. We are coming of age through education; when we demand good industrial products, no designer can deny them to us.

Many small-size industrial products such as tools, kitchen utensils, radios, etc., can be brought to the classroom for examination and discussion. But if this is not possible, illustrations from magazines, books, and newspapers will provide a contact with contemporary industrial design. At the lower levels, the basic concepts of the criteria should be explained and adjusted to the experience and maturity of the group.

Photo courtesy Dux.

Courtesy IBM Corporation.

Courtesy Rosenthal Block China Corp.

Courtesy Aluminum Company of America.

Courtesy Dansk Designs.

Courtesy Aluminum Company of America.

Courtesy Aluminum Company of America.

Courtesy Celsa Corporations of America.

Courtesy G. Jensen.

62

Children's toys—courtesy Fred Bassetti.

Arches against the sky, courtesy Herb Edmands.

Children's toys, courtesy Fred Bassetti.

The interior of a typical guest room of a Japanese home illustrates the sensitivity for proportions and the free flow of space uncluttered with furniture and accessories. To the Japanese, beauty and utility are synonymous whether in architecture or in the tools of everyday life. Design and quality of craftsmanship are maintained. Courtesy Japan National Tourist Association.

The Visual Machine

Sculptors have always been interested in movement which seems to give life to their materials. In the past, as among the ancient Greeks, a raised arm, twisted torso, or a turned head, gave the impression of bodily movement but it was left to the mind to interpret the gesture as movement. Actual movement has only recently become a studio problem. Given springs, shafts, cogs, and wheels—all materials from the salvage yard, the inventive artist constructs a machine which can tick, whirl or spin in space. Because this is an age of movement characterized by the dominance of the machine, the moving sculpture becomes an appropriate symbol of our century. When sound is added, the impression is complete.

In any moving sculpture, no matter how interesting the movement becomes, mechanical operation must cooperate with visual appearance of shapes and colors. When all the elements of the visual machine are in harmony, the composition becomes a complete form.

Charles Stokes, the youthful artist of these visual machines has this to say of his work, "I have tried to make fun of machinization, but frankly my machines are not as funny as the atomic bomb. As I finished each machine, I became aware of an insidious reflection of myself and all humanity in them. The machines resemble humanity so much—they are wound up, started, go a little bit crazy for a period of time, then they stop. A significant cycle indeed."

Courtesy Charles Stokes.

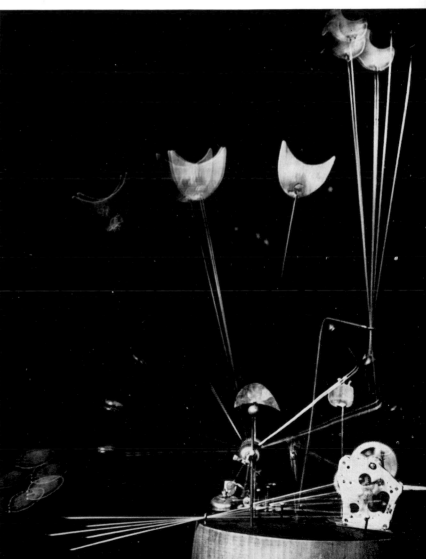

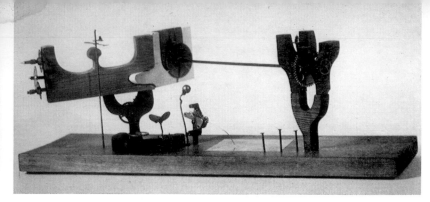

1.

In the rhythmic movements of nature, the mobile builder has discovered a problem of universal interest. The mobile, or sculpture in motion, is especially appropriate for our century because it requires materials of our time: steel wire, nylon thread and plastic. In addition it is directly related to our interest in movement. Materials for the classroom mobile may be cardboard (painted with oil-base paints), thread, wire, and balsa wood.

3.

2.

1. A visual machine with a minimum of moving parts taken from clocks. The action is simple as the spring unwinds with a soft whirl. Parts of this machine do not move but are intended to add visual interest. Areas of bright color are added also. Courtesy Charles Stokes.

2. A vertical mobile with both moving and stationary parts departs from the usual ''arm'' type which Alexander Calder made popular. Each disc is brightly painted. The material is soft-soldered wire and wood. Courtesy Charles Stokes.

3. A combination of stabile and mobile is made of wire, sheet metal, and glass which tinkles in the breeze. The Oriental wind chime gave this artist his idea. Household cement holds the threads securely to the glass.

Some Suggestions for Teachers

LEVEL	AIMS	MATERIALS	KINDS OF PROBLEMS	NOTES
PRIMARY	To satisfy the urge to build. Encourage unconscious articulation of space; familiarity with ideas of 3-D design to expand child's conception of a 3-D world	Construction toys, building blocks, cardboard play houses, clay, paper, blunt-end scissors, paste, string, soft wire	Exploration of space in gardens and large and small rooms. Modelling in clay, paper, sculpture, papier-maché. Tours	Large muscle control with increased ability to refine motor activities; no technical information required at this level. Teacher's role to provide material, assist in fastening, cutting. Give encouragement
ELEMENTARY	Conscious articulation of space; building with space blocks for purpose; increased awareness of esthetics of space; use of simple vocabulary. Awareness of citizen's role in city planning; preservation of nature. Use of tools, hand and jig-saw; problems in construction; awareness of good design in industrial arts	Above materials plus balsa, cedar, etc. All hand tools. Glue	Mobiles with basic problems in achieving balance. Model homes, simple machines, modeling in the round, relief construction, clay modeling pottery. Tours	Ability to use fine muscles, take advantage of child's interest in movement, discussion of design in autos, homes, etc. Many children have mechanical ability
JUNIOR HIGH SCHOOL	Relate to growing interest in opposite sex, the home, social events. Encourage thoughtful approach to art and extend use of vocabulary. Take advantage of romantic interests in foreign lands and exotic arts	All materials, including stone carving, casting, plastics	Stress crafts of practical value, pottery and ceramic sculpture, jewelry, etc.	Take advantage of interest in detail and fine skills
SENIOR HIGH SCHOOL	Advanced vocabulary, study of major architects and their philosophies. Stress emotional connotations of space, home furnishings and design	All materials	Attempt to break the hold of realism; to explore contemporary theories	Refine consciousness of history and contemporary life, lives of great artists. Research in current magazines and books. Establish relationship between specific culture and its arts

Some Three-Dimensional Problems

Using some of the three-dimensional materials mentioned below, many of which are interchangeable, construct a space composition involving some of the following problems. Several problems may be combined in one.

1. A solid three-dimensional form (mass) which invites physical (sensuous) as well as visual inspection. Create interest with shape, textures, and light and dark. *Materials:* oil-base clay, ceramic clay, plaster, or carved wood (balsa), soft cedar, mahogany, etc. *Levels: EJS*

2. Construct a composition with toothpicks, straws or other linear material and fast-drying cement utilizing the concept of transparent planes. Add cellophane or gelatine for color. *Materials:* natural or colored toothpicks, straws, twigs. *Levels: EJS*

3. Construct a relief with plywood or cardboard in which planes project into space at various depths. Add color and texture, perforations. *Materials:* plywood, packing boxes, cardboard, glue, scissors, etc. *Levels: EJS*

4. Using two-dimensional material, create a composition which strongly states the direction of the planes involved. Planes stating direction may be larger, darker, textured, etc. Use subordinate directional planes also. Relate problem to architecture, building complexes, or interior space division, gardens, etc. *Materials:* plywood, cardboard, glue, etc. Caution: do not use water-base paint on cardboard which warps. *Levels: EJS*

5. Create a transparent mass with string tensions over wire form. Suspend a mass within to add interest. Soft wire may be bent into rigid geometric shapes such as a box, or curvilinear, spherical shape. *Materials:* nylon, string, yarn, soft wire (aluminum or heavy gauge copper wire, baling wire, etc.). *Levels: JS*

6. Using cardboard boxes of various sizes, construct a geometric relief with both positive and negative shapes. To strong background glue cardboard boxes (some faced down), perforate and string with yarn. Unify compositions with light-dark pattern. Employ spherical shapes or cut paper to intensify interest. Paint if desired with oil-base colors. *Materials:* cardboard boxes, heavy background of cardboard or plywood, yarn, cut paper, plastic balls, etc. *Levels: JS*

7. Construct a sculpture consisting of curved planes of paper or cardboard in which the negative dominates. Suspend shapes within. Perforate if desired. Add additional volumes to complicate. Subject matter may be animal or human motif. *Materials:* construction papers, paste, string, etc. *Levels: EJS*

KEY: E—Elementary; J—Junior high school; S—Senior high school.

Bibliography

General Design and Appreciation

ART: SEARCH AND SELF-DISCOVERY, James A. Schinneller, International Textbook Co., Scranton, Pa., 1961

ART TODAY, Ray Faulkner, Edwin Ziegfeld, Gerald Hill, Holt, Rinehart and Winston, New York, 1963

DESIGN: A CREATIVE APPROACH, Sybil Emerson, International Textbook Co., Scranton, Pa., 1953

ELEMENTS OF DESIGN, Donald Anderson, Holt, Rinehart, and Winston, New York, 1961

UNDERSTANDING THE ARTS, Bernard S. Myers, Henry Holt and Co., New York, 1958

Sculpture and Three-Dimensional Arts

ART IN MODERN ARCHITECTURE, Eleanor Bitterman, Reinhold, New York, 1952

CONTEMPORARY SCULPTURE, Carola Giedion-Welker, Wittenborn, New York, 1960–61

EXPERIENCING ARCHITECTURE, Steen Eiler Rasmussen, Wiley, New York, 1959

GARDENS ARE FOR PEOPLE, Thomas D. Church, Reinhold, New York, 1955

ORIGIN OF MODERN SCULPTURE, W. R. Valentiner, Wittenborn, New York, 1946

SCULPTURE OF THIS CENTURY, Michel Seuphor, G. Braziller, New York, 1960

SCULPTURE OF THE TWENTIETH CENTURY, Andrew Carnduff Ritchie, The Museum of Modern Art, New York, 1952

SPACE, TIME, AND ARCHITECTURE: THE GROWTH OF A NEW TRADITION, Siegfried Giedion, Harvard University Press, 1954

STICKS AND STONES, Lewis Mumford, Dover, N. Y., 1955

THE ART OF HOME LANDSCAPING, Garret Eckbo, McGraw-Hill, New York, 1956

THE ART OF SCULPTURE, Herbert Read, Faber, London, 1956

TRADITION AND EXPERIMENT IN MODERN SCULPTURE, Charles Seymour, Jr., American University Press, Washington, D.C., 1949

Magazines

ARTS AND ARCHITECTURE . . . CRAFT HORIZONS . . . INTERIORS . . . DOMUS

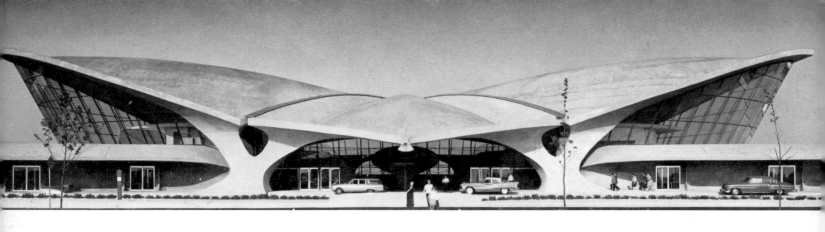

TWA Passenger Terminal, Kennedy International Airport; Eero Saarinen, Architect.

Photos, Ezra Stoller
Associates.

70

Philharmonic Hall, Lincoln Center for the Performing Arts, New York City.

Above: Emperor's Palace Gate, Kyoto, Japan. H. Armstrong Roberts photo.

Left: The Harbor Observation Tower, Rotterdam, The Netherlands. Ewing Galloway photo.

Below: Restaurant, International Airport, Los Angeles, California. H. Armstrong Roberts photo.